COLOMBIAN ADVENTURES

A True Missionary Story

Based on the Book *Rescue the Captors*

Russell M. Stendal

Copyright © 2016

Illustrator: Monica Bruenjes
Editors: Sheila Wilkinson and Ruth Zetek
Paperback ISBN: 978-1-62245-314-6
eBook ISBN: 978-1-62245-315-3
10 9 8 7 6 5 4 3 2 1

ANEKO
PRESS

Our Readers Matter™

www.AnekoPress.com

Early Childhood

Do your parents ever tell you to wait until you are older? Maybe you want your own phone – or a computer – or a bicycle – and they say, "Wait until you are older."

Have you ever gone to the fair, and they said, "You can't go on that ride. You're too short. You need to wait until you are taller."

Did you ever look at an airplane and wish you could be the pilot? Or fly a helicopter?

Sometimes it is hard to wait so long. Fun, exciting things happen when you are older, but getting older seems to take forever. Russell Stendal felt this way when he was very young. But then, something amazing happened.

In 1957, Russell was a talkative two-year-old who lived in Grand Rapids, Minnesota, with his parents. His father, Chad, was a civil engineer who worked on big construction jobs like bridges.

Russell was interested in everything, and his mother taught him about God. One day he asked her, "Where does God live?"

"God lives in heaven, but He can also live in people's hearts," she replied.

This sent Russell's mind spinning. "Does He live in your heart?" he asked.

"Yes."

"Does He live in Daddy's heart?"

"Yes, He lives in Daddy's heart too."

Then Russell asked about friends of his parents and their children, but his mother wasn't sure about their youngest child. She told Russell that a person must ask God into his heart. Russell thought about it and then asked, "Does He live in my heart?"

Russell's mother did not know what to say. She thought he might be too young to understand this deep spiritual truth. She told him, "When you get older, you can ask God into your heart."

That was not the answer Russell wanted. He slid off his mother's lap, knelt beside the bed, and prayed in a loud voice, "Come into my heart, Jesus. Come into my heart, God."

Then he stood up, jumped up and down, and exclaimed, "He's in there! He's in there!" His mother did not know what to say.

During this time, Russell's mother read many stories to him. One time when he was three, she read *The Three Little Pigs* to him. It was a fine story, but at the end, the wolf ended up in a pot of boiling water with its nose sticking out from under the lid. Poor Russell. He loved dogs and that wolf looked an awful lot like a dog. He was so upset that his mother decided to read only Bible stories to him from then on.

Russell loved the Bible stories. He would jump on his rocking horse and pretend to be a traveling preacher.

One night when Russell was four years old, Mr. Stendal came home from work and plopped Russell on his lap to show him a big, colorful picture book about the Indians in South America. Mr. Stendal liked to teach his son about new things and places. He wanted him to learn about people all over the world.

The book showed the Indians working and making crafts to sell for money. But it also showed the Indian men taking the money and drinking in the saloon while the women and children waited outside. Sometimes the men argued and fought with machetes. At the end of the day, the women would help the men get home to sober up for work in the morning.

Russell was shocked to realize that people lived like this in the beautiful Andes Mountains. "Why do they live like this, Dad?"

"Well, Russ, I guess they don't know better," his dad answered.

"Why don't they know better?"

"I guess no one ever taught them or showed them a better way."

Russell became indignant. "Why hasn't anyone gone there to help them?"

"I guess it's because no one really cares about those Indians, Russell."

Russell looked up at his dad and said, "You care, don't you, Dad? Why don't we go?"

Mr. Stendal didn't know what to say. He had a fine job that paid a lot of money. They were very comfortable in their home. Finally, he said, "Well, Russ, a person can't just take off for a foreign country. That would be a missionary's work. God would have to call you and provide the finances to prepare the way. Maybe when you grow up, you can be a missionary."

With that, Mr. Stendal settled back in his seat, thinking he had heard the end of it. He thought he was off the hook.

Russell, however, had climbed off his dad's lap and knelt by the couch. Russell prayed. Russell prayed in a loud voice. "Dear God, please call my parents to be missionaries so I won't have to wait until I grow up."

Mr. Stendal became quiet and thoughtful for the rest of the evening. That was 1959. Eventually, he resigned from his job, sold their house, and applied to Wycliffe Bible Translators.

Linguistics School

The Stendals soon needed to register for language school, but they only had enough money for Mr. Stendal. It cost $15. When Russell heard that his mother couldn't take classes, he gave her $15 from his own savings.

In June of 1962, the family loaded their small car and a U-Haul trailer. They drove to Grand Forks, North Dakota, and were very tired from the long trip. Even worse – Russell was carsick and had been vomiting on the way.

They arrived at the University of North Dakota where Russell's parents would study how languages are formed. Russell's father went inside to check in. It took a long time, and Russell and his brother, Chaddy, and sister, Sharon, were getting restless. They had been stuck in that car for too long.

All at once, Russell turned white. He opened the car door and threw up on the street. Little Sharon took one look and vomited all over the front seat and her mother's dress. The car reeked from the vomit, so when Mrs. Stendal told Chaddy to go find his dad, he flew out of that car.

After the family settled in, the parents went to classes and the children were able to have swimming lessons in the pool at the university. When Mrs. Stendal got a "C" on the first quiz, Russell told her, "I paid my money to send you to school here. I don't want it to be wasted."

From then on Russell helped with the younger children so his mother could study more.

Jungle Camp

The next summer the family headed to the southern part of Mexico for Jungle Camp. This three-month camping trip sounded exciting – and it was, but . . .

The family lived in a one-room hut, but sometimes they took trips into the jungle. Then they slept on hammocks with waterproof netting over the top. Staying right-side up all night turned out to be tricky, and when Russell flipped his hammock, he had to call for help to get straightened out.

At Jungle Camp they learned about dugout canoes,
  water safety,
    and riding the rapids.

With special permission, Russell went on the long canoe trip even though he was only seven. The co-director did not like this idea, but the director said it was okay.

They were assigned a short, tippy canoe with a large woman to go with them. Mr. Stendal thought the leaders wanted them to capsize and force Russell to go back. However, as they rounded the first bend in the river, they saw the overturned canoe of the leader. He and his passengers were floundering in the water as the swift current swept Russell's canoe past them.

When they stopped for lunch, they noticed that all the other canoes were wet inside. They had all capsized. Everyone was wet except Russell, his dad, and their passenger, and many lunches had washed away downstream.

One time they hiked twenty miles into the jungle to the Advanced Base. The children rode mules and the mothers and fathers walked. Sometimes the mothers rode for a while with the children. When they arrived, they were glad to crawl into their hammocks for the night.

But poor Russell.

He had nightmares that night – all night long.

Every time he felt the hammock move,

he dreamt he was on a horse and it was tipping over.

Advanced Base was where they learned more survival skills. When Russell needed penicillin for an infection, the staff member told Russell's mother to give him the shot. Everything went well.

The next day when they returned for another shot, the staff member was gone. Russell's mom was alone, and Russell was not sure about this. Mrs. Stendal promised Russell a *Sugar Creek Gang* book when they got home if he cooperated.

Ouch!

The first attempt didn't work because the needle was bad. Mrs. Stendal changed the needle, but Russell did not want another shot, so his mom promised him another book.

Ouch!

The needle jammed again. In the end, Russell left with a sore bottom and the promise of four books.

The jungle was one adventure after another. Russell went with his dad to an Indian village and slept on a straw mat in an Indian's home. He gathered wood chips for fires and played in the river on a raft. He and Chaddy made their own snail soup on their own fire. This was a little boy's paradise.

When Jungle Camp was over, the family passed all the tests. After one more summer at language school, they were ready for Colombia.

So, in January 1964, at 2:00 in the morning, they were flying over the Caribbean Sea. Russell looked out the window and said, "We're really having fun, aren't we, Dad?"

School in Colombia

In Colombia, Russell was not happy in school. He could not understand his teacher because
   she spoke Spanish,
      and Russell did not.

Mr. Stendal bought Russell a Spanish-English dictionary and taught him all the Spanish sounds. Russell took it to school to help him.

A few weeks later, Russell came home from school at noon. The teacher had taken the dictionary and demanded that Mrs. Stendal return to school with Russell to speak to the principal. The teacher claimed that Russell would not obey, and because he read perfectly out loud, she thought Russell understood Spanish perfectly. After they explained that Russell knew the sounds but didn't know what the words meant, Russell did better.

Later, Billy Townsend came and stayed with the Stendal family. The two boys went to Lomalinda with its rolling hills and valleys where Mr. Stendal was building a base for the missionaries. They slept in hammocks just like at Jungle Camp.

Mr. Stendal gave them their school assignments to do while he worked on the construction projects. He said he used the bait-and-switch approach to school. If they did not do their work, they got the switch. If they did it, they got a piece of candy.

Russell and Billy were smart young boys. Mr. Stendal reported later that he never used the switch, but he was running very low on candy.

When the boys finished their schoolwork, they ran free in their tropical paradise. They carried water from the lake and washed dishes. They made friends with the locals and became very good at Spanish.

They swam and accumulated pets –
   parrots, monkeys, and toucans.

The Indians taught them how to hunt and fish. The boys learned about the land and thrived with the freedom.

First Plane/Chaparral

After high school, Russell went back to Minnesota to study agriculture and get his pilot's license. He returned to Colombia in 1975 to help his dad with some farmland they had purchased. They called their farm Chaparral.

They wanted to use the farm to help the Colombians improve their lifestyle by teaching them modern farming techniques. The people were so poor that Russell was uncomfortable sharing the gospel without also helping them live better. They hoped Chaparral would help the people.

The land was cheap because it was far from the city. They had to build roads, houses, airstrips, and fences. But the Colombians did not work very hard.

They wanted to sing and pray all night. They wanted to hunt and fish. But they did not want to work hard in the daytime. Some left the project because they did not think educated people should do manual labor.

Before long, Russell realized they needed a plane. His friend had been injured and needed to get to the hospital. A pilot in the area said he would fly him to town, but needed to be paid first. It took a day to get the money, and Russell's friend almost died.

Russell promised God that if he had a plane, he would never turn a person down if they were ill and had no money. Soon after that, he heard a plane. When it landed, he ran to see who was flying in to the area. Out climbed his dad and another friend.

When Russell asked whose plane it was, his dad said, "It's ours." Russell looked at the old, underpowered Cessna 170 Taildragger and thanked God.

When a Pig Flies

In those early days of the ranch, they needed money for supplies and food. One day Russell flew to the ranch and found Chaddy and his crew desperate for food. They wanted him to fly straight back to town to get supplies, but they had no money for the groceries.

But Chaddy had an idea. He said he'd "take care of everything."

Chaddy showed Russell a big, fat pig –

the biggest pig Russell had ever seen.

Chaddy said, "We'll tie the pig up,

load it in the plane,

and you can sell her in town and get supplies."

Russell was not sure about this, but he took the passenger seats out of the old plane. Chaddy told him he worried too much. "We can tie all four feet together in a knot that I guarantee you will never come undone. Besides, this is a tame pig. It knows us."

It took all of the men to lift the 250-pound hog into the plane. Russell closed the door, strapped himself in, and started the engine. The pig was lying on the floor –

grunting once in a while.

Russell thought it might work. As he taxied down the short airstrip –

Whump!

The pig flipped against the baggage compartment,

broke the partition,

and slid into the tail cone.

The plane could not fly with so much weight in the back, so Russell closed the throttle and prayed that he would be able to stop before the end of the runway.

He did.

Barely.

Russell undid his seat belt and pulled the squealing pig out of the tail. All four feet were still tied. The men helped get the pig in a better position. Russell looped the seat belt from the co-pilot's seat between the pig's legs and cinched it down.

This time the take-off was perfect, and soon Russell and pig were at 6,000 feet headed for San Martin. All was well and Russell settled in for the 90-minute flight. The pig grunted and squealed, but Russell got used to it.

Then, all of a sudden –

Ka-whump, ka-whump.

Horrified, Russell saw that the pig had pulled its back feet out and was banging the side of the plane with its hind end. Ka-whump again and the door latch broke; the rear end of the pig slid out the door and dangled in the air while its front feet were still connected to the seat.

The plane started to turn sideways as the pig struggled to get out. It stretched and stretched –

trying to touch down –

not realizing they were 6,000 feet in the air.

Russell got out of his seat and pulled as hard as he could. He pulled and pulled. The plane was flying without a pilot and started turning. But Russell could not get that pig back in.

Then an idea popped into his head. Russell reached over to turn the plane and bank it the other way to lift the pig enough to get it back in.

The plane turned;

    the pig fell back inside,

        but she landed on top of Russell.

Together they slid to the other side of the plane and broke the latch on that door.

Now Russell was pinned under the squealing pig with the door open. He madly beat on the pig to get it off. The pig was so upset she doo-dooed all over Russell.

Peeeee-U

The stench was really bad. Russell grabbed an iron bar and hit the pig. She went berserk.

She got up,

    she thrashed,

    she squealed,

    and she gnashed her teeth.

Finally, after getting kicked a few times, Russell tied her down again.

By this time the plane was shuddering and shaking. Both doors vibrated and flapped in the wind. The whole frame shivered.

Russell tied the left door with the end of the rope from the pig's hind feet. Then he held the right door with his right hand and flew the plane with his left.

He sat on his right foot so the pig could not bite him and handled the rudders with his left foot only. Then he prayed.

Finally, they got to San Martin, but as Russell was going in for the landing, he saw donkeys in the runway. He had to do a go-around and try again. Pig was getting upset again. Russell buzzed the donkeys to get them to move.

They just stood there.

Russell had to do several passes before a boy came along and got them off.

Somehow, Russell managed to land the plane with one hand. The butcher gave him $100 but the new latches for the doors cost $120. Russell learned to think and plan before doing something like that again.

Captured

With the airplane, Russell and Chaddy decided to start a wholesale fish operation. They bought fish from the nationals, froze them in a large walk-in freezer, and flew them to town. They hoped they could make enough money to pay for all of the emergency flying that Russell was doing.

The Cessna 170 flew supplies in and fish out. Russell flew back and forth and back and forth with fish. The little plane was creaking and moaning from old age, but Russell did not have money to buy a new one. However, one day the plane quit three times on the way to the farm.

Instead of buying a new engine, Russell let the salesman talk him into buying a new plane,

a bigger plane,

a Cessna 182,

on credit.

Russell and Chaddy owed a lot of money, but the fish business was good, so they thought they could pay it all back.

But the next month the dry season started. The fish sank down into the cool mud and waited for the rainy season. In the deep river, fishing got very slow. The bills piled up. Then after the rainy season started, problems with the mafia and drug dealers made the fish business expensive and dangerous.

Guerrillas invaded the area and shot up the Cessna 182, so one day Russell and his friend Gilberto flew the Cessna 170 to Canyo Jabon for a meeting with Carlos and some businessmen who wanted to buy some of the equipment from the fishing business.

Carlos met them when they landed, but they heard gunfire. Carlos said it was nothing to worry about. They went into his store for the meeting. In a very short time, Russell saw armed men running down the street. This made him suspicious. He carried a 20-gauge double-barreled shotgun, but that would not be enough against so many.

The armed men called everyone into the street. Carlos and Gilberto went out, but Russell waited inside. Soon Carlos came running back and told Russell to come out also. Russell hid his gun in the store and stepped out.

Russell stared at three machine guns pointed at him. "March!" they told him.

So he did.

Attempt to Escape

They marched into the jungle and told him to lie down. Russell thought they might shoot him, but a man named Manuel pulled his arms behind him and tied a nylon rope around his neck and arms with a slipknot to keep him from running away.

Russell worried about the gun he had strapped to his ankle. His pant leg had pulled up, and he was afraid the guerrillas would see the gun. However, they didn't, and when Russell stood up, he tugged at his pants and covered the gun.

They marched farther into the jungle until they came to a river. On the riverbank was a large pile of military equipment, backpacks, and a large canoe. Jaime, the leader, came over to Russell and told him he had been kidnapped. He asked Russell if he was armed.

Russell lied.

But the guerrillas went through Russell's bag and found bullets. Russell lied again and said they were his brother's. Nancy, who was the nurse, came over and was taking Russell's blood pressure and heart rate. At that time, Russell faked a heart condition and told the guerrillas to stop bothering him. Nancy sent them away.

Three times Russell had lied.

Then they climbed into the canoe and headed up river. As they went around a bend in the river, they saw a boat. Fearing it was the police, they pulled over and pushed Russell to the back of a banana patch. The others prepared to ambush the police.

Manuel grasped the rope that was around Russell's neck and kept his submachine gun pointed at him. He took Russell farther into the jungle, but when shooting started at the river, he turned his head to see what was happening. At that moment, Russell grabbed the gun from his ankle holster. He aimed at Manuel's right shoulder, hoping to disarm him so he'd drop the rope.

But when Russell moved,

Manuel jerked back.

Russell fired, but hit him in the chest.

It knocked Manuel down, but he held the rope tight. It was choking Russell and cutting off circulation. Russell shot again and tried running, but he was dragging Manuel along. He took shelter behind a tree.

By this time the guerrillas were coming. Giovani aimed his German assault rifle at Russell and pulled the trigger.

Click.

Nothing happened. It had misfired.

Russell aimed at Giovani;

pulled his trigger – nothing.

He was out of bullets. Giovani was trying to reload behind a tree as Russell was scrambling and dragging Manuel with him. He checked his pockets for more bullets. He was choking and knew Giovani would follow. He was at the end of the rope.

Russell lowered his head and waited to die.

Into the Jungle

Instead, the guerrillas retied him – much tighter. They threw him in the canoe and covered him with a tarp. Russell's arms hurt from the tightness of the cord, and a nail was poking him in the back. Then it started to rain; Russell was wet, cold, and miserable.

Manuel lay beside him. He did not look good at all. Russell was afraid he might die. He was afraid they would torture him for shooting Manuel.

So, Russell prayed for Manuel.

When they pulled over to the riverbank, they set up a mosquito net for Manuel, and Nancy worked on him. At nightfall, they picked up their gear and hiked farther into the jungle, single file. Three guerrillas went first, then Russell with Arnuvel holding the rope, then three more guerrillas. Nancy stayed with Manuel. Later a jeep came to pick up Manuel and take him to a field hospital.

When they stopped to rest, Giovani told Russell he had never had a gun misfire before. Both men agreed that God had kept them alive. Giovani also told Russell he had not been tortured because Manuel should have searched Russell and found the gun. Russell realized that the guerrillas respected him a little for his courage, but they were also quick to judge and kill.

He decided to be very polite.

Later in the night, a Russian jeep met them and took them to a place for a camp. They unpacked hammocks with mosquito nets and tarps. They guarded Russell all night. While Russell shivered from the cold and damp, the guard sat holding the nylon cord and pointing a machine gun at him.

Camping with the Guerrillas

In the morning, Giovani brought Russell some coffee and gave him breakfast. Russell sat on a damp log while the men sat around cleaning their weapons. They talked and joked. Russell told them he had to stand up for what was right because he was a Christian. He told them that kidnapping was wrong, and he had an obligation to resist. He said he had not tried to kill Manuel. He just wanted to wound him so he could escape.

Later, the new leader, Vicente, came. He was a negotiator and wanted money in exchange for releasing Russell. Nancy also returned with news that Manuel had had surgery and was recovering nicely.

At dark, they moved again and set up camp along a river. This became a more permanent camp. Jaime cleared an area for Russell and furnished it with a bench made from poles and vines. Alfredo built him a table, and Giovani hung Russell's hammock with the mosquito net. Jaime also brought him a wool blanket. All this time, Arnuvel held the rope and pointed the gun at him. Eight guerrillas were assigned to guard Russell.

These guerrillas talked and played chess. They were friendly until Russell talked about politics and world issues. The communists had taught them to hate Americans, and they believed all of their troubles came from corrupt capitalism.

It rained a lot and the campsite was ankle-deep in mud. Then it turned sweltering hot. The guerrillas continued to guard Russell every night. The guard would lay his flashlight alongside his gun so he could shoot if he needed to. Every time Russell saw the light on him, he knew the gun was pointed at him with the guerrilla's finger on the trigger. It made him afraid he would be shot accidentally.

After breakfast in the morning, Russell exercised. Alfredo made him a bar for chin-ups, and they found two gunnysacks to put on the ground for sit-ups and push-ups. Russell paced back and forth as far as the rope would allow. He thought about his wife and baby daughter at home, and that depressed him.

Russell tried to see God's purpose in this situation. He wanted to know how to present truth to these guerrillas. He admitted his lies were wrong. He had learned from Giovani that atheism is the basis for communism, and they considered "religion" a crime against the people. Russell spoke with Giovani about God and evolution, communism and creation.

Russell started writing everything that was happening to him as a way to stay focused, and his writing began looking lengthy enough to become a book. The guerrillas made Russell a desk and put a tarp over it. Mariano gave him a typewriter, and Arnuvel announced that Russell would type his book in Spanish for all of them to read. When Russell typed, the captors leaned over his shoulder and read along.

Vicente took pictures of Russell to send to his family to prove that he was alive, as they negotiated for a ransom. Russell's mother sent him a Bible.

Sweet Tarts

One day Russell got a package from home that had some candy – those giant sweet tarts.

He took the purple one out and ate it,

smacking his lips

and exclaiming how superior candy from the United States was.

He ate the whole thing;

then Russell took the red one,

broke it into pieces,

and offered it to his captors.

They enjoyed that red sweet tart. Then Russell stood, smiled, and exclaimed, "I win; that candy had poison in it. You will die in five minutes."

Looks of terror spread across their faces. Mariano pointed his gun at Russell and declared that if he died, he'd kill Russell also. Russell went back to typing. Five minutes passed. Nothing happened. He told them they were okay, but "now you can see that terror is wrong."

They did not think Russell's joke was funny, but Russell started seeing his captivity as an opportunity, not a disaster. God had a purpose. Russell was to be a witness to these atheists. He told them peace and freedom came from mercy and love, and mercy and love came by ending rebellion against God.

Russell learned about these guerrillas – their lives, their hopes, and their fears. He even found out that some wanted to leave the guerrillas and go home, but they could not. They would be killed if they did. They were trapped.

Guerrilla Headquarters

After 67 days of captivity, Russell was transferred to the main guerrilla headquarters. Hundreds of guerrillas were in this camp. They tried to brainwash Russell and told him that they had captured his wife. They were lying, but this was very upsetting to Russell.

But many of them talked to Russell about the world and God. They talked about the peace that he had inside. When the leaders found out that some of the guards were interested in God, they transferred those guards to another place and made Russell's life miserable. They wouldn't let him sleep and gave him strange-tasting lemonade to drink that made his head hurt. They were afraid of Russell's book. Some of the men were beginning to think there might really be a God.

Russell continued to tell them about God and forgiveness and challenged them to consider God. He offered to show them around America so they could see for themselves that it is a good country with good people.

Release

After 142 days in captivity, three of the guerrilla guards came running to Russell. They quickly took down his hammock and announced that he was to be released. They took off through the jungle, and then blindfolded him for a five-hour boat trip. Finally, they pulled over, removed the blindfold, and took the rope off. Russell stepped out and saw his brother Chaddy and two negotiators.

Chaddy had given them some money, but the men wanted more. Chaddy and Russell had to agree to pay as soon as they could. Then one of the men told Russell he had heard about his book and gave Russell permission to keep working in that area.

The guerrillas returned his wallet, his watch, and his bag. Russell gave something from his bag to each of the guards and shook their hands. Mariano was last. He was sobbing and asked Russell to forgive him for the way he had treated him.

Chaddy and Russell traveled up the river in a speedboat to a small town where they spent the night. The next day their father flew in with the repaired plane. They let Russell fly it home. First he buzzed the airstrip, and then he took the plane up and enjoyed his freedom.

Epilogue

What is Russell doing today?

Afther his release, Russell travelled in the U.S. and Canada with his wife and daughter, but God had instilled in Russell a love and concern for the guerrillas. He went back to Colombia to distribute Bibles and literature.

In 1998, he started his first FM radio station, broadcasting from Lomalinda. Today he has about 12 different radio towers and is able to transmit throughout wide regions that are difficult to reach otherwise.

These transmissions have led to invitations to "events" inside the guerrilla areas. In this way, Russell can distribute literature and Bibles. He also distributes solar-powered radios that are preset to one or two of his stations. With the success of these radio messages, Russell looks to expand to the Colombia/Venezuela and Colombia/Ecuador borders.

Russell still flies planes too. In fact, he does parachute drops. With these, he is able to drop Bibles, literature, children's books, and radios in the most remote areas. Hundreds of thousands of parachutes have been dropped.

Russell's daughter wrote, directed, and produced a documentary film about one of their adventures with the fighting factions. Russell uses this movie, *La Montaña*, to open more doors in Colombia to the gospel.

In January 2013, Russell began travelling to Cuba to interact with the government of Colombia and the guerrillas as they work toward peace. Russell still has enemies, however, and he was recently arrested because some think he is a terrorist, even though he only works for peace. But he is free today and continues to work to obtain freedom for fellow believers and share the peace that only God can give through Jesus Christ.

Scan to watch a video update from Russell

Watch the La Montaña trailer, a film based on a true Stendal adventure

Connect with Russell's Ministry

Website

www.spiritofmartyrdom.com

Receive newsletter updates

http://goo.gl/amBsCD

Buy books

http://amzn.to/1nPLcNL

CPSIA information can be obtained
at www.ICGtesting.com
Printed in the USA
LVOW05s0334220317
528011LV00005B/5/P